T0149837

CANE | FIRE

CANE

SHANI

POEMS

FIRE

MOOTOO

BOOK*HUG PRESS
TORONTO 2022

Contents

III

My mother was an Anglican
My father was a priest
Together they prayed real hard
When spring came (and the Pitch Lake overflowed)
They reaped the smoothest stones you've ever seen

Did Water Fall?

It was definitely not the rock-a-bye kind of rocking
nor did the world
gently swing.
I believe the ship's bells
clanged. Of course
I would have wanted
sanctum
in her hands. The lights winked.
I winked back.
When she cried out, so did I.
No one sang.
I thought I heard, *When the bough breaks*.
More likely, she'd have asked, *Will the bow break?*
He did not say, hush. Or laugh.
The water jug on the dresser trembled.

I always hear her

          scream

               my name.

Veranda

From city eaves dangled Jack Spaniards' papery nests

like schoolboys' term tests, crumpled

tossed and caught in the black-painted

wrought-iron garden

that rose above rows of pots

of curly-leafed

bread-and-cheese begonia

lushly fringing

the wraparound

black-ledged veranda

and though your belly was full

                        of cake and milk

you pressed each shell-pink pillow of begonia

for a soupçon smear of yolk-yellow citrus sour

and waited

and as you waited, you contemplated

                        mechanics of de-stinging

                        principles of taming

red-bellied yellow-banded Jack Spaniards

then slowly, below, begins the babbling

and the flow

you crouch behind your potted jungle

                and watch

the charm of girls in green skirts and white blouses

glimmer through the latticed doors

of a white-walled madrassa

whose golden star and crescent moon

shine brighter than heaven's own stars and earth's own moon

and you marvel

at how hummingbirds know

why the muezzin sings

and why at this time on the street below

white-capped men in white dresses flow

Heaven's Own Stars

Darkness climbs stairs
                    seeps under doors
            night in a dress reeks
                            patchouli and fire
                shadow mischief crawling

                cloven-hoofed lajabless
                        crouch in corners

                He tilted my face
            to the butchery bloodshot sky

                behind his back, my finger
                looped inside his belt

                                (which he sometimes removed
                                coiled around one hand
                                its pointed tongue snapping
                                the other's open palm)

Faraway thunder low-rumbles inland
sheet lightning   tic   tac   toes

                The waistband of his pants
                    warmed my hand

                                Those were days rain never fell

To lajabless, soucouyant and jumbie, he was salt

Look! his index finger pointed
Quickly wish, wish you may   Quickly wish, wish you might

But what wish
wish for what
he was all
everything, enough

A True Story about an Unreal Marble

after-lunch heat cripples a butterfly
galvanized roofs creak and ping
confetti of cane ash blankets the town

from Empire Cinema
three blocks back
a sitar hunts

a woman pleads

to the midday-still argent clouds
that crown Sutton Street's
exalted concrete and front-garden house

in the front room
a wilful child is made to rest
atop Tide-scented hummingbirds
iridescent green, hibiscus red

but

the wilful child herself

takes flight:

through the window

up Mucurapo Street

past the abattoir (she pinches her nose)

to where turbaned vendors adorn Library Corner

banishing last night's gutter-piss and broken bottles of booze

with foreign-perfumed foreign grapes

and apples wrapped in purple paper

back in the room on Sutton Street
below the open window
passersby jiggerty jig
with baskets of provision and fig—
chittery-chattery-envy-admire
Ma's bevy of fuchsia poinsettia

when shade releases the street corner
big boys gather on her grandfather's factory floor
and play pitch with bags full of pretty marbles

the wilful child, eyes closed, rubs her cheek
up-down her grandmother's pale and ample
upper arm

from the corner bureau whorl lullaby-scents—
cananga, khus khus, cedarwood, bergamot

until she finds the crimson keloid twistable marble—
arm-nipple to suckle

(twisted off
            it could be
                        a big taw
                                    with which
                                                to pitch
                                                            on the
                                                                        factory floor)

under the wobble-whirr of their ceiling fan

the wriggling wilful grandchild
searches for that keloid thing
the thing on Ma's upper arm

                    finding it, she sucks
                        then ventures

                        a little bite

Ma's brow furrows, eyes shutter-flut
It hurts, baby, don't do that
Rock-a-bye baby

                A wilful child learns to wait

until Ma's eyes are still
then she tries again

suck the keloid big taw
consider when and how to sever
such a thickened scarlet scar

of course, I'd keep it safe
rolled between my fingers
hidden beneath my tongue—

my very own big taw
with which to pitch

and show big boys how to score

Inventory

the cabinet door snaprattles   open

       limebayrumOldSpice

snaprattles   shut

silver mirror   old confidante

                        winks back

                        eyes to knowing eyes

                        his tortoiseshell pocket comb

                        rakes his thinning hair

in the bedroom he slides open the dresser's top drawer

       eucalyptusthymesandalwoodlimementhollavendercamphorclove

she leaps on the bed, all the better to see

he shoves in the drawer—   *There's nothing in there for children*

                          go outside and play

* * *

the daily paper spread, his map
of the world, soccer and the odds of this and that
condensed into columns and tables

down which he drags a foot-long ruler
to underline in Bic red
the curious and misspelled

he nods, or shakes his head
at the brown and gold wall-mounted radio's
commentators rehearsing

new words for a new republic:
constitution, independence, prime minister
governor general, privy council

the woman who in real time bakes
begins an upside-down pineapple cake—
he turns the volume down low

then up again—loud
for the broadcast of yesterday's
FA Cup Final

***

the dresser that holds nothing for children

glows

what child doesn't need

a peerha of her own?

to reach

wood handles smooth as skin

whisper-pulled

just a crack

and there

eucalyptusthymesandalwoodlimementhollavendercamphorclove

Pull again

but...

pull harder then

manage yourself on the peerha

and pull push yank

***

Vick's inhaler   dollars cinched in a gold-plated pin
purple-edged white handkerchief   a pen
yellow and red Three Plumes *Don't play with that!*

slide open sniff the crumbly brown sulphur heads

hair pins   safety pins   paper clips
pretty blue Optrex cup   greasy bottle of Vicks VapoRub
copper pennies *That's dirty take that out of your mouth!*

pressed to her lips
a ventured lick

salt and blood

penknife *Put that down now!*

the blade's stuck, won't come out

Bic ballpoint pen   sharp-pointed pencils
Don't run with that in your hand!   teal and gold pretty bottle 4711
                    mustn't mustn't mustn't

                sneeze

bottle of hair oil   many-sided jar of Tiger Balm *Put that down—you
want to burn your skin, or what?*

grey dust clinging to a strand of hair

a penny   stuck
won't budge, glued perhaps   to the floor
of the drawer
even a fingernail can't pry it up

tie pins   a farthing   silver cigarette holder   half crowns
florins   shiny brown pearls in a brown bottle

don't smell like chocolate but make a good chac-chac

tin of Phillips Milk of Magnesia   pencil sharpener
a nail file for prying up glued pennies

from the home office

   the long scrape of a chair pushed back—
    the radio has been turned off
    the radio has been turned off
    the radio has been turned off

  drop the nail file close the drawer—push shove

    push, lift, push harder

  the washroom door squeals open, closes, a stream
     hits the water

wriggle this side, shove pull lift up down up down
the dresser trembles a bottle of pills tumbles the toilet flushes
heart thunders
kick the peerah under the bed

follow the peerah

FAST

Rocking Chair

for Mike Gaudaur

high above, full-on glitter

                        red and yellow black and white

adrift on the veranda

                        they are precious in His sight

I assign to the stars

                        let me hide myself in Thee

buzz song of the cicada

                        oh, this little light of mine

curled in his lap

                        close beside me all the way

sleep comes easy

                        nothing in my hand I bring

Limacol and Vicks

                        little ones to Him belong

rise off his shirt and skin

                        they are weak but He is strong

rhythmic weight of his foot

                                                 my tears forever flow

sustains the off-kilter

                                              when upon life's billows

of the bentwood rocking

                                              watch me where I lie

in and out of soft tungsten

                                            His shining throne on high

we teeter

                                            wash me Saviour or I die

his anise breath

                                              tempest tossed

tenors

                                            sins and griefs to bear

through my hair

                                            be of sin the double cure

Answer

Did I or didn't I myself

see the jar

    or was it a jug?

                distinction relevant

                memory manifest

                was it an escarpment of logic

                a story told

                falling

                falling

                never

                landing

                pit or pith or brick

                of origin(s)

        did water fall?

                if so, then (so)

                humbug in my bones

                cervical vertebrae

                perennial vise of ice

                in equatorial heat

                foreknowledge

                of icicles

                              still so drawn to water

                              drawn to cold

my mother: water?

                           oh, you mean

                           water

                           well, actually there was, yes

                           water

                           there was that day

                           everywhere

                           water

                           but you must

                                       how many musts does it take
                                             to blunt a knife
                                             to wash a brain
                                           to chase the chaser
                                    that chased the chaser that chased
                                                    the chased

                           ...nevertheless

                           you must

                           understand

                           a storm on the crossing

                           north to south

                           the boat

                           skidded   rocked   rose   fell

pause

pause
and weigh

water water
everywhere
spilled sloshed dripped
yes, the side of the crib

your father
me, both of us, yes, both
wiping water wiping

and how, why now you shiver so

you must

but

brick of origins
rhymes with gut cut nut clutz mutt butt disrupt must

know it wasn't our fault

how still you bear that shock

drawn to water drawn to cold

everything isn't

always

our

fault

beware the outsider who tries to penetrate

he shouldn't look   wouldn't me

on the left of his left
on the right of her right
in the middle of the left
to his left her right
on the right his left
on her right her left
on his right his left
her middle his right
his middle her left
the right of her right
on the left of her left
in her middle his night
in his middle the left
on the left of her right
she had the right
who was right what was left
left right left he left
in the middle of a night

didn't touch   couldn't see

Fine

White

Line

Barely

Visible

Line

White

Fine

Honour

Thy

Mother

And

Thy

Father

Buried

In

Fine

White

Linen

Fine

White

Line

Barely

Visible

Line

White

Fine

Honour

Thy

Mother

And

Thy

Father

Buried

In

Fine

White

Linen

OUTLINE: CHILD RESEMBLES FATHER---SO FAR ALL IS WELL--
--BUT ONE DAY CHILD ACTS OUT----FATHER WARNS CHILD--
--CHILD ACTS OUT AGAIN-----FATHER BANISHES CHILD---BUT
CHILD LONGS AND LONGS FOR-----A LEG LEFT BEHIND AND
THAT SORT OF THING-------SO SO AND SO CHILD CLIMBS
MOUNTAINS----CROSSES GLACIERS----HIGH HIGHER HIGHEST
--COLD COLDER COLDEST---EATS WORMS AND GLASS AND
ANDER ANDEST--- GROWS THE LARGEST PUMPKIN EVER
RECORDED---BUT BUTTER BUTTEST--FATHER SLOWLY
REMEMBERS CHILD'S NAME NAMER NAMEST

everyone devotes themselves to trying harder and harder
after which
and then but even so and how the Pitch Lake flooded

41

Beware

the insider

who tries

to break

out

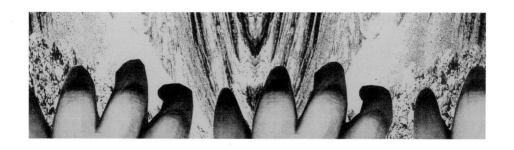

The Smoothest Stones

The audience
wanting a stoning
offered the podium—

Punish who
banish you
clownish him
mannish her
follow us
shun them

They brought with them their own
plates of black cake and silver buckets
of palm-sized stones

Amazed, I asked
Can you not see
I *am* him

...when to do otherwise would bring down the wrath of a wedlock into

unconscious desirability, of leaving an entire leg behind)

which one is born and from which one forever tries

bursting forth (not ever really appreciating the inevitability, perhaps even the

a man's child lays her father bare / picks the flesh off his bones /
leaving a skeleton as white and empty / as that of a fish / ~~preyed on~~
prayed on by vultures

Legacy

for Naila DeSouza

Kamarband, wound and wound about the waist, multi-tasking sash, essential of the Indian man, flamboyance quotidian—brow mopper, money holder, grocery/letter carrier, pants cincher, dagger hider

In translation, stationed in India, British army man's borrow-theft–cummerbund—close, yes, and best with a cigar—heat mitigator, attribute enhancer, camouflager of imperfections in the aspiring man—conceals unflatterables: tuxedo shirt's bunching buttons, wobbly bellies, rolling bands, too-tight trousers. Its upturned pleats from artless lips indiscretions catch, and secret legitimate—certainly illicit—calling cards.

To explain—with pride and hilarity—my grandmother's white skin, this one line: great-grandmother, married to one Mr. Mathura, was the British estate owner's concubine.

True or false?

A minor detail: kamarbanded Mathura with his bibi crossed the Kala Pani from his namesake province in Uttar Pradesh, birthplace of monsoon-cloud-blue Lord Krishna, where men like Mathura, and women like my great-grandmother—stars in their honeyed eyes—are straight-nosed, poised and pale—long preceding any goddamned 'cross-the-kala-pani estate owner.

True or false?

At formal dinners and dances, Bibi's Trinidad-born grandson outshone imperialist proprietorship of the ladder-climbed cummerbund.

Does a photo even exist

of rotundo rotundus rotund, stout yet lean, Uncle Ralph—
Indo-Trinidadian pantheon
not smiling?

I, knee-high to a fly, from the arched veranda observed: single-
buttoned jacket dinner-jacket black, silk lapels, bow tie to match,
shirt bright-bright light-exuding white, silky black stockings and
mirror-black shoes. Wavy hair patent-black, forehead garnished
with provocative curl. Before getting behind the burled wheel of his
burgundy Jaguar, Starboy, ring-adorned hand, smoothened upward
the pleats of his elevated MathuracityinthestateofUttarPradesh
waistband. On leather heels honey-eyed he spun—and voilà—a flash
of dash—burgundy velvet-silk cummerbund.

Sleeping Dogs

The little

p

i

e

c

e

s

to which one clings

cut crystal bowl, dented lid tarnished   silver

once contained your rose-and-citrus-scented body powder

a catch-all now for nuggets of scattered time

buttons   rudraksha seed   shell of limpet

beads

ceramic   glass stone   plastic

half a bangle   earring   inch of plumber's chain

watch face   red, white and black beetle pin   big taw marble

fragments of yellow-yellow gold

Every day, Christine feather-dusted the pair of terriers

VINTAGE, SYLVAC, POTTERY

MATERIAL: CERAMIC, COLOUR:
GREEN, 5", USE: DECORATIVE

STARTING BID: NFS

Yours since you were a child on Sutton Street
(what kind of child, pray tell, is given and keeps ceramic dogs for pets?)
(did they travel with you all the way to Ireland and back?)
airlifted after, as they say, *you left*

leave me once
shame on you

leave me again
and again

shame
on you

from your dresser
in Bel Air to rest atop mine
two thousand five hundred and forty miles away
Swiffered biweekly in Prince Edward County by Christine North

Chipped ear
noses glisten black
ceramic's thin thuck answers the fingernail rap

I had rather hoped, in the echo, your breath
and the exhale of my name

everything
veranda, roof, railing
eventually crumbles
dust to dust

on auspicious days the watch I wear is your handclutching my wrist

fortitude in life you couldn't give, imagined

you accompany me
tame every trepidity

The silver dinner bell sat

the silver dinner bell sits

the silver dinner bell will one day

Is it true we'll meet again?
what if?

Mightn't I rather just keep right on
hailing
glorifying
missing

eternally elusive you?

The Crick in the Crack

the signature ingredient
an axe applied with force
to the anterior fontanelle

a metaphor to temper truth
quell libel
is an angle

that softens which, and whose blow

four three two one ready or not here I come

time was

                                      crick crack

the "champagne of soft drinks"   angel cake   Jesus Loves

in our blue-black diamond-studded night

                    Michael rowed his boat ashore

        Saturday mornings, beggars stooped on the cement
ground floor

        Ma and Barlow placed one wrapped roti and a shilling
in open palms

                       go upstairs

        one o'clock two o'clock three o'clock four

time was

crick crack

my grandmother's breast

was my Eden of plenty and rest

her innate, forever prescience—

a dowser that outdoes water

—divined the depth of this paralytic lung

say your prayers

time was

                                                                    crick

today is not a day to run, darling. Walk

round and round the room she ran

in her periphery, the long shiny box

and the wailing woman named Mummy

                                                                    crack

round and round the steamy room I swam

breath held like an unmasked diver

I trawled for a leak on the ocean floor

                                                                    crick

one behind the other, mourners filed

white kerchiefs pressed to lips

round and round, she saw

each one's fingertip slide

down the side of the shiny Ma-length box

that separated them from the passed

                                                        turn out the lights

faster, faster, round and round

her breath-held canter

couldn't stop Pa

or the man called Daddy

or Humpty Dumpty

or Frank or Barlow

or Jesus of the Rock of Ages

from that long hard lid drawing down—

they're all suffocating Ma

                                              say good night

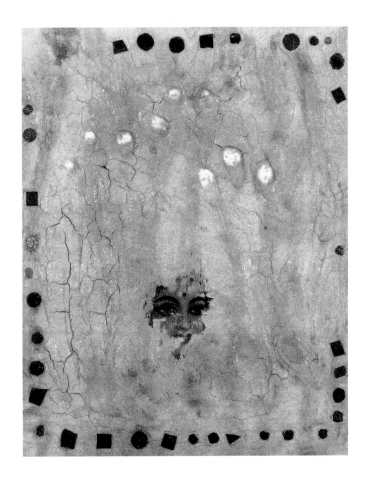

latía a un ritmo de mi corazón
louder, louder

her eyes

                          closed

must mustmust mustmustmust mustmustmustmust

up the hill and round the bend
people lined the street
heads bowed as the hearse passed and the two cars travelling at 10
(not even a dog barked)
in head-to-toe black the funerary march
on heat-softened asphalt
delivered a measured beat

at the rear, Saturday's beggars donned sheets
bleached-white and pressed

rock-a-bye baby, on the treetop

the sun shone down, as if
nearer my God to Thee
cars went by roadside, as if
even though it be a cross that raiseth me
in the distance schoolboys chattered and yelled, as if
still all my song shall be
birds in the samaan above us came, went and squabbled, as if
nearer my God to Thee

Reverend Chankersingh rocked on his heels and said something
though like the wanderer the sun gone down
Pa stood back
darkness be over me
the woman named Mummy screamed
my rest a stone
I dared not
yet in my dreams I'd be
the thud of dirt, scattered across the shiny wood
nearer my God to Thee

when the slackened ropes swung
the man named Daddy caught the fainting woman named Mummy

when the wind blows, the cradle

is a ladle

full of holes

Oh, the phantom axe (remember?)

crick crack and all things fontanelle

time was

                                        crick crack

oh Mummy, I wore the crinoline for you
look, over here, we're back here, waiting for you
oh Mummy, I embroidered this tea towel for you
move away from the window, Mummy
from the phone, the cigarette, the knife, the gun, the door

oh Mummy, I'll play psychologist
friend, eye, lawyer, mother, father
mouth and man for you

                              there's a crick in every crack

concrete and rebar shook

                                             crick

a dress ripped preserved
like Chinese salted prunes
is evidence or a souvenir?

                                 was i or was i

                                 i was, wasn't i

a pet cobra likes to be stroked

        but must be milked
        of their poison at least three times a day

                to blame

in the end, do children keep their mothers alive?
if so then (so)
does she curse the children for keeping her alive?

                for the women

                   he was

                   seeing

from the twisting samaan of
life—would he stay or go?

                   crick
                   crack

      in the dark, wide-eyed, children wait
        for the tank-size hum and moan
      of a Mercedes as it creeps round potholes

   to the left to the right in the middle of the middle of the night

              monkey breking back

       for nutten but a small-small piece a pomerac

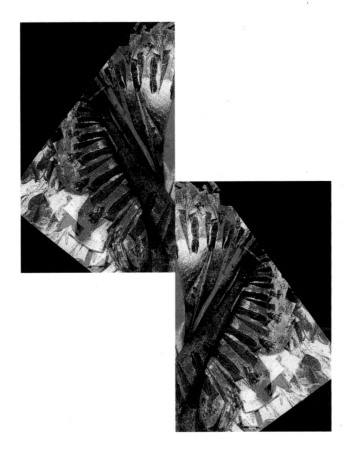

but he brave for so—what he have in mind coming home with so much lipstick, like a misplaced boutonniere, on the collar of his white office shirt?—not so he is the one everybody love as he always giving away hundred per cent discount on everything-everything?—lights turn off, and he coming inside singing loud-loud, oh what a night, what a night—she waking-waiting, but time she hear that car is in the bed she jump making like she sleeping—the children, too—his friends, incredulous, laugh and warn, you know you must know and rehearse your alibi well—is a monkey what does brek he back for nutten but pomerac

time was

                                              crick crack

                              Huckleberry Finn and I
                                rafted down the M
                                      I double S
                                      I double S
                                      I double P
                                             I

                                        into whom
                                   was impregnated
                            possibilities for escape
                            before understanding

                                      true escape

                                 is an a priori imp

                              o s s i b i l i t y

time was

                              crick

a set of encyclopedias
equals the weight of a human heart

                      and magically

quells the forever-loading gun

A to Z, Z to A

Zygophyllum: genus of the monogynia order
belonging belonging begloling begonling boloning globoning gblonging

to the decandria class of plants

A: the name of several rivers in
various parts of the big wide world

                              crack

a conch shell to my ear to hear
nothing
but the outermost most rare

                              crack

on repeat, Oh Very Young
taught/taunted before I'd barely begun
I'll only be dancing
a short while

so run

faster than a cheetah
high high high
higher
than
Rüppell's vulture

like a butterfly I beat back gale-force winds and listen for her voice

it is she, isn't it, who screams on repeat

Where Are You Now, My Son?

                                                                crack

            the crick and the crack of that anterior fontanelle—

                                                        despite
                                                        despite
                                                            how
                                                             it
                                                            had
                                                            all
                                                        begun

—promises my mother
has always
been looking
for me

but couldn't always see
I
was
I am
her boy
who every day
walked, walks
ran, runs
flew, flies
across muddy battlefields
upon which we once were, are forced to lie

                                                    crck crck

'crick

in Barbados

your leg
tucked
between
mine
when the tide—
the frilly spitting waves
and only
shells

kelplike
you swayed
salt
tug and pull
the gentle slam

how strange
to hold your hand

certain as moon and sun
that seventh wave

      the sea—
    birthing water
folded in on itself

angled holes
appeared
in the shoals

I lost my shoe

grasped your hand
as if it were breath

and anchored my heels
into the sliding sand

crack
crick

and
I
was
am
the girl
she couldn't see
rafting up and down rivers far from her and home
who I could and couldn't, without her, be
explorer of the how
and what
I like
to do
and have done
to me

no matter how far
I'd roam

no matter how long from home

I am the girl

she didn't see

casting petals round her feet

crack

a mother's pursed lips
standards set
Fridays she gets her hair done

Scottish Mrs. Flora Willis lived up the road and smelled of English lavender. She was hired to make me comprehend algebra, the subjunctive and the moving parts of a triangle—failing this, she taught me, instead, the art of Japanese ikebana and introduced me to *Epiphyllum oxypetalum*, the night-blooming Cereus, the latter word derived from Latin, wax, waxen, waxy, pliant, easily swayed or persuaded

my father notices people's nails
dust in corners and rain spots on his car
for a party of ten he hires a bartender

nowadays he talks about me
to his friends

and tells the same tales, gen an agen

it ends, it always ends

i'd like to have stood
like him

on the hood of the car
that floated down the Ortoire

at the restaurant
he asks the singer
to sing to me

his favourite song

i'd i'd ticed
early long ago
if my edges ran parallel
they clapped kissed popped corks poe
harder they they capped, the arrower I glew
th narrower i thruw% thegroleur and yet i ,,, (deborgdt
thk' as;h a;song 2;ashhh to al I I afhhth, =-> a tha; and yet, and yet
how i love it y eihrn hr dmilr sy mr, the smile that broke the camel's back

When

—more apt than if—

the word *truth*
dissipates

sugar in rain
an unused limb

so will the declaration:
lie!

Is THE assault on truth assault
if those (of us) on whom it is enacted

suck our teeth

admittedly
in a kind of despair

and acquiesce
        and acquiesce
                and acquiesce
                        and acquiesce
                                and acquiesce
                                        and acquiesce

Drawerful of Time

Was I
and therefore am?

But when there is no one in the forest
what harm in   recomposing

Photographs were, in any case, blurry

Apportioned, chiselled words evoke
wedges

something akin to something
scattered across the dreampillow

seashell shards tossed up in the foam
a fold in time, my river flows upwards

My river flows
backwards

Close enough has to be close enough

Some time ago, my mother told me
thedominoesplayer had died

Oh no, said I, *too bad, I'd like to have killed him myself*

No, not that one, she answered, the other one
I asked her to convey my condolences

Later, on a visit back home
I came across "the other one's" youngest daughter
and

                    forgettingforgettingforgetting

    in a single breath asked

How'syourdaddoingthesedays?Irememberheusedtoplaydominoeswithmygrandfather

Pupah's Estate

For Arini Wingson

On the stove steam rose

from the pot of first-milk

of the cow that had just given birth

Colostrum

she explains

to which was added

the curdling juice of a lime

half a cup of cane sugar

a teaspoon of ginger

a pinch of nutmeg

Morning milk, she tells me, is different

than daytime milk

and both from nighttime milk

During the first growth spurt

the baby wants her every ten minutes

The turbaned workers alternating hands

        pull   pull

            pull   pull

Rhythmic squirts pinged the metal pail

white froth and foam rising

        Even when it feels like there is nothing there

            the baby just pulls and pulls

The house smelled

sweet like a human baby's mouth

What was the name of that town again?

You and I love your sea, rock for all ages, Bathsheba; sand of brittle
pink pelts down to the troubled salt surf, I drop to my knees, slide
long and clean into the spitting foam—a backward glance in hopes
she saw the skin of my shins, raw, how they bled for her; he sang
Michael row the boat ashore while we each vied to be first to see
the sliver of silver shimmer behind the grove of *Cocos nucifera* under
which wild crocus grow; the red swing's ascent and descent, the
tickle in my nipples, from there to the vagina a juiced cord strummed,
hallelujah—let's do it again; growling Alsatians finally lay down and
let me pet them; so you hear how a 24-hour lizard run up she shirt?
But she wasn't no Teacher Mildred—and hysteria fuh so! Almost make
she dead; Aunt E. imagined we couldn't hear when she farted—we
acted as if we hadn't, but one by one, from the room we departed;
onions and garlic wafted up off her dark brown fingers that held the
glass of pulpy orange juice to my lips; yes, it was I who followed close
behind as you marched down the hallway and dove into your bed—at
the foot I stood—remember?—and made my point—you pulled the
blanket up over your head and said, please; in the early morning light
Macho the Pomeranian, plastic cone around his neck, danglefloats
just below the surface of the backyard pool; my thundering heart at
the window—first ever sight of snow; my face distorted in teardrops
of ice from each red chokeberry in the blue-white snow; first ever
crack of ice, Victoria Glacier booming, Lake Louise below; the first
touch, your soapy hands on my bony back; the first taste of who I was
and what I wanted to be, she arced her back—touched my head with
both hands—she said my name preceded by oh; and yet, oh yet; the
beginning and the end of my story, the first scent, ice-cold scotch on
his breath, sung through me his rocker-chair hymns.

The Inevitable

What my eyes see

Theatre

of Desire

I Dream of

Doing

The Way You Bounce Off a Pane of Glass

Moments used to be

       Far

                and
                few

                        between

Now they line up

A continuous stream   of

                        dots

The sea fizzes, so far   s   o far you go

Tal   king
of tomorrows

I'll sleep when I'm dead

Two thousand five hundred and forty miles

Upon her tongue the phantom marble twirls
in foreign's beds
absence stretches
full-length beside her

The cane-ashed town, ticklish lover
jealous custodian ablur in sepia

Nights, she bolts upright, skin sticky with recall—
the window open no air aswirl
the Syrian his bicycle   the bell bellowed his wares—
olive oil   ylang ylang   clothes pins   vetiver

A sari flutters in the sky
loop-de-loops
disambiguates the sitar's drone

On her side of spear-tipped fences painted silver, pink poinsettia
on the other side, the silver-haired drunk man, a handsome man
wailed for his glass-eyed mother

Blind birds flew through cane-fire sweetened air

Between thumb and forefinger
a phantom of marble, crimson air
out of the wound of night seeps chimera

Absence, a clever lover, supine beside her

Waiting and Not Waiting for Mitsuko

She always slept on the left side of her bed

Switch up country, city, house, apartment
seasons of lovers wait, love is a sign worth parsing
circumspection in the tryout, revealing

Take note of the new flame who lays claim to one particular chair
helps herself to the same mug more than twice
and, given two clothes hangers , takes five

Of the owner of the toothbrush that travelled overnight
from prone on the ledge of the sink to upright
inside the wall-mounted toothbrush holder

Having stayed over, two nights in a row
she took it upon herself to water the plants

much too soon

Come on, I mean really, is plant-watering such a big deal?

(all landscape exists in the decision to stay or go
the request to stay or leave)

she came   and went
in the thick of night   through the back
                    door

the prowler encountered several other prowlers
all looking in the same corners for the same bundle
of straw

***

Two thousand five hundred forty miles
and change
twenty thousand four hundred forty days

or so

hours, minutes
and counting

***

That she hadn't sat in the same seat at the same table
two meals in a row
is all that sunders then from now

***

~~A woman~~ The woman wore a not quite black Japanese-styled jacket
a piece you'd think Mitsuko Uchida might wear
her hair, a halo of fire

spun on her heels, said something

What was it she said? Something about classes of mangoes
the ruse of Proust's cattleyas, purple petals arranging
on bare heels a powerful pirouette
the twist and flick of her hand, an arrow sprung

and, well, just like that

***

Grocery bags hang off the front door
her blue velvet chair, left side of our bed
the microwave-safe oven-proof Woodland plate: Majestic Deer
the meaning of life is approached between
contemplating dough hydration percentages and
studying rows of heirloom lettuces from the back door

I AM WRITING A FIRST PERSON narrative set in the present
Family and friends regret they cannot be present
Phone calls from Seattle, London, San Fernando, Vancouver
are a present

Climbing up out of the cellar

List of clichés:

we finally

silver bead-studded buttercream-frosted **chocolate cake**

become

on either side of the cake silvered glass vases

more constellation

from which spirea fountain

than consolation

cascade

in the city living room gather
fourteen deerlike witnessing family   —who knows what
they really think?—and puckish friends whose
thoughts contain us

I cried when I read the vows

You were beautiful, even if dazed
a glass of Veuve Clicquot
rosettes of mashed potato
scallops gratinéed

Some strange force took control

and trembled our hands

when we signed   certifying normal

Sometimes I Call You by My Father's Name

***

The foundation
never actually sets, the past
oozes from the pore of every stone

sweet and (s)our blood

old knowledge lurks

bearing weight these bones

Once Upon a Time

***

father, mother, sister, neighbour,

wouldn't a
couldn't a
shouldn't a

cognizance is a kit, the wary and the
waiting set in ħHome

Sunday lunches in the dining room
chatter and laughter
sitting right there wishing to be more there than there,
on her left, on his right, in the middle

we pleaded: you said
today, he answered
no, I said *tomorrow*
which, we cried, is
today
but didn't I say, he said,
tomorrow

in the back seat of his
car

cold cigarette-smoke-
flavoured air huddled us
together

even if it poured, it was
the best
day of the year

it is a small miracle I do
not call you by his
name

***

in his house
we sleep together
in the same bed
he calls us both *Love* and introduces us to his friends
at dinner he regales us with questionable jokes and pours red wine

***

when I call you by my father's name
a small miracle, then

you and I are family

We'd Always Intended to Test the Well Water

I was fine, until you came along, my dear
Once upon a time, no one dared say, *no way, move over, lower, higher*
But things have changed, and now, that you may go first is my
    dreaded fear

I'll be the madwoman scratching dirt for the birds and music we share
We whittled to I, who will rewrite our anthem: *together we aspire?*
I was fine until you came along, my dear

In this race, which of us will shed that first tear?
If you're not here to say—*goddammit, you didn't—again—turn off the*
    fire!?
For so many reasons, the possibility that you'd go first is my greatest
    fear

Write out where the keys and passwords are--I will never remember
Who is owed, what to expect, when and what will expire
These duties I did just fine, until you came along, my dear

But I've since forgotten how. And what if I were the first to go, who'd
    take care
Of *you*, change the battery, call the plumber? Would you hire yourself
    a new driver?
Nevertheless, that you could go first remains my greatest fear

The birds will still call your name, not mine, but it is I who will be here
Your love for them will keep me from turning this house into our pyre
I was fine, until you came along, my dear
But things have changed, and now, that you could go first is my
    dreaded fear

Inhabitance

The star magnolia over Frankie
Is not Frankie
The tree, now fifteen feet tall reaches farther
Leafless to the May blue sky
She is not Frankie
There were lofty reasons for placing her
Above the rosewood urn
But she isn't Frankie
In a breeze her thousand ear-like petals canter-dance
But no, not Frankie
Each strokable incandescent bloom
Uncannily akin to Shih Tzus' silky hair
Does not mean she is Frankie
In sunlight her silver incandescence
Oddly, smells of groomer's whitening shampoo
You would not have liked those little insects on you, would you, Frankie?
My heart, amazed at how perfect my choice
Sinks back to that time before, and I remind myself
A tree is not a dog, is not Frankie

Her unselfish bountiful display will last to the end of the week
Then be gone until same time next year
Would it have been kinder, Frankie, to set us both free?
Her petals will wilt and brown, fall to the ground
Do I cane myself or honour you, Frankie?

Suddenly, I see I've missed again
The cherubic beauty of a star magnolia

She hadn't meant to be anything but her majestic self

On Christmas Day

the old man across the street

dresses to the hilt in his kilt,

sporran bobbing on his waist

he struts across Main Street

and brings us bottles of his homemade Cabernet

this nectar, this friendship
bend it toward   my face
liquid cool and sweet

the flower still on its stem. I stoop
and squeeze into my mouth

Staff of Love

Your

Bread

she said

Makes

Me

she said

Want

to

R

o

l

l

Around

on

the

ground

and

W   h   i   m   p   e   r

Acknowledgments

The County of Prince Edward where I live is the traditional land inhabited by the Anishnaabeg, Wendat, and Haudenosauneee Peoples and is adjacent to the Kanien'keha;ka (Mohawk) community of Tyendinaga. I am deeply grateful to be able to live and work here. At the heart of the long story told in the poems in this book Cane | Fire is a solid core of a handful of people who were there at the beginning. If it wasn't for them, I might well not have made it, or I might have made it with many more holes in me. Dhanmatee Samaroo née Mathura, Deoraj Samaroo, Indra Mootoo née Samaroo, Ralph Samaroo and Estella Bhoodosingh remain part of me. Barlow and Frank were there, but in my world in those days they didn't have last names. Nevertheless, they made me laugh and cry, they caught me before I fell and, at times, Barlow at least attempted, but I must say in vain, to have me disciplined.

Those who catch me now, in every way, including the catch in holding one's feet to fire, are Deborah Root, Indrani Mootoo, and Vahli Mahabir. They and Shelagh Hurley, Marlene MacCallum, David Morrish, Jane Howard, and Naila De Souza have been anchors in love and in friendship and in conversations about art, writing, storytelling, friendship, family, and love. Shelagh and Marlene have read various drafts and made invaluable comments along the way.

About Deborah Root—this writing and artmaking thing I do, she makes easy and immensely pleasurable for me. It is deeply satisfying that I feel this way about her own artmaking, too. We push one another and only grow because of it. I am a lucky person.

The first iteration of the book had me struggling on my own to translate the project as I saw it in my head onto the page. But one thing I learned over the years, particularly as a video artist and photographer, is that there's always someone better equipped to help you flesh out and bring your ideas to life. Michael Gaudaur of Quinte Studios in Trenton, my friend and photography printer, was the master

121

I turned to for that initial support. He had only a few times to say, "Are you really still asking if it's possible to do something? Come on, let's do it." And he'd work his magic, making invaluable suggestions along the way, a process I enjoyed tremendously

I am very fortunate to have Samantha Haywood of Transatlantic Agency on my side and want to thank her and the Transatlantic team for their ongoing support and advice.

My publishers at Book*hug Press linked me up with people who "felt" *Cane|Fire*, who "caught it", at once. Sandra Ridley is one of those. *Sandra Ridley edited this book.* I state this fact simply, because I am in awe. Sandra would ask a seemingly easy question, the kind of question that stumps you because of that very straightforwardness. I'd turn my head. What meaning, I'd think? I'd go away, ponder, and come back having realized, and appreciating, the depth and wisdom in every encounter. Out of this particular work relationship it was inevitable that a friendship would grow, too.

Cover and book designer Gareth Lind is another. His immediate and uncanny understanding of what I wanted to do with and in between images, words and spaces that are the paper page itself, blank but not blank, was remarkable. Nothing was compromised. Everything is as I needed it to be. There is the book design, and then there is paying attention to the tiniest of details of the writer's wishes, and Gareth's obvious passion and immense talents made this writer-artist's dream come true.

You read the manuscript a thousand times, your friends, too, and you all make corrections, and still, the copyeditor comes in at the end and finds enough to make you so very grateful that he and his talents were there. Thank you, Stuart Ross.

The final product, in this case this book of images and words, seldom resembles the first tentative submission, especially when, like a child with a new drawing, you excitedly send it off, half-finished, raw, as yet more idea than work. After sending the manuscript to Hazel Millar and Jay MillAr of Book*hug Press, with whom I had already had an amazing experience with my previous book, I went to Costa Rica for a three-week holiday. It was there that I received an email telling me that they had accepted the manuscript for publication. One never gets used to this kind of news. I can't thank Hazel and Jay enough for taking on this project—made deceptively simple-seeming because of the talents and expertise they brought on board—and for so generously providing me with all that was needed to make *Cane|Fire* a reality. I also want to acknowledge all the very smart and important work Jay and Hazel do on a personal level, and via the platform of Book*hug Press, in the field of publishing in general, and specifically for writing, writers, and readers.

About the Author

Shani Mootoo was born in Ireland, grew up in Trinidad, and lives in Canada. She holds an MA in English from the University of Guelph, writes fiction and poetry, and is a visual artist whose work has been exhibited locally and internationally. Mootoo's critically acclaimed novels include *Polar Vortex*, *Moving Forward Sideways Like a Crab*, *Valmiki's Daughter*, *He Drown She in the Sea*, and *Cereus Blooms at Night*. She is a recipient of the K.M. Hunter Arts Award, a Chalmers Fellowship Award, and the James Duggins Outstanding Midcareer Novelist Award. Her poetry has appeared in numerous journals and anthologies, and includes the collection, *The Predicament of Or*. In 2021 Mootoo was awarded an honorary Doctorate of Letters from Western University. Her work has been long- and shortlisted for the Scotiabank Giller Prize, the Dublin IMPAC Award, and the Booker Prize. She lives in Prince Edward County, Ontario.

Colophon

Manufactured as the first edition of
Cane | Fire
in the spring of 2022 by Book*hug Press

Edited for the press by Sandra Ridley
Copy edited by Stuart Ross
Design and typography by Gareth Lind
Typeset in Classic Grotesque

Printed in Canada

bookhugpress.ca